Grass in Green

Collected Poems

by
Tasneem Hossain

Grass in Green

Collected Poems

by Tasneem Hossain

Grass in Green

By Tasneem Hossain

First Edition

Author: Tasneem Hossain
Editors: Paul Gilliland and Shirleen Manzur
Formatting: Southern Arizona Press
Cover photo by Former Korean Ambassador Yun-young Lee

Published by Southern Arizona Press
Sierra Vista, Arizona 85635
www.SouthernArizonaPress.com

ISBN: 978-1-960038-06-7

Poetry

Preface

This world of ours is fascinating with all its grandeur. Everything around us has a story of its own. These stir my imagination. As I get immersed in them, sudden outbursts of emotions give rise to a myriad of thoughts and reflections. Words start gushing out like water from the fountain and then gather in a pool creating musical waves; giving birth to my poems.

Poetry to me is divine in its own light. Poetry immortalizes a single moment or a vast expanse of kaleidoscopic views of a certain aspect or aspects of life.

This book is a journey through life's different moments: sometimes beautiful, sometimes bitter; sometimes spicy, sometimes sweet, sometimes sour and sometimes hot.

In a world full of chaos and complexity the title poem *Grass in Green* speaks of harmony: harmony between individuals, communities, countries, and different religions. Mutual care can give birth to a new life of happiness, peace and prosperity.

The years 2020-2022 shook the world with COVID-19 pandemic that turned the world upside down. Our personal lives had a roller coaster ride with isolations, lockdowns, deaths, heartaches, loss, fears, and failures. The poem 'Merciless' and 'Another Sunrise' speak of the devastation it created: both end with a note of hope. 'Fractured Rise' is about domestic abuse and gives courage to fight against injustice and ends again on a positive note. 'Break the Bias' and 'I will not accept defeat 'are strong affirmations for gender equality. 'I am a Prostitute' creates awareness in society. Many of the poems are about love in its purest form, even if it is unrequited. The greed and misuse of power are themes of some poems like,' Pawns in the Game'. Some of the poems speak of the inevitable uncertainties of life and inspires us to recuperate and be strong to embrace the inevitable changes and jump back to life again with vigour.

This book is an amalgamation of different reflections of life: Positivity being at the centre.

Dear readers, I write for you. The success of this book remains in your experienced hands

Tasneem Hossain
January 6, 2023

Acknowledgement

Writing is one thing and compiling a book are two different things. A book is truly rewarding but writing a book is harder than I thought. It became easier for me with all the steadfast support of my family and friends.

I extend my heartfelt thanks to my daughter, Shirleen Manzur, who not only inspires me but has helped me shape many of my poems with her constructive feedback. She was incredibly supportive in helping me develop ideas and has helped me in editing the poems for the last 18 months. Shirleen, though you are my daughter, you will always be my guardian angel.

My gratitude to my husband Manzurul Islam Chowdhury for all the sleepless nights he spent to give me company, while I wrote. His adulation acts as a strong motivational force. Thank you for always being at my side

The relentless support of my son, Nafis Muntasir, and his witty remarks always fuel my imagination to go an extra mile. Thank you son: you are special.

Thank you Sabrina Zaman for your constant praise of my poems.

The constant encouragement of my brother, Col. Asiful Hossain, makes me yearn to write more. I remain grateful to you.

There is an enormous group of friends whose constant praises and admiration stimulate me to keep writing. To name a few: Farhana Hossain, Shamima Haque Chowdhury, Zahida Sattar, Lubna Yusuf , Syed Reja Ali, Shakeela Baker…. The list is too big to incorporate everyone's name. Friends, I believe you know who you are. Please know that you all occupy a special place in my heart. I thank you all from the core of my heart.

Mr. Paul Gilliland, how can I ever thank you enough? Thank you for having faith in my writing. You have constantly been in touch with me with your generous assistance in furnishing me with all the tiny details of what works and what doesn't. I remain grateful to you.

My special thanks to Southern Arizona Press for formatting and publishing this book. Without their support, this book might not have seen the light so soon. I wish you all the best for the future.

My readers play a huge role in intensifying my passion for writing.

You, my readers, are the reason that I write. Thank you for being there.

Tasneem Hossain
January 6, 2023

Contents

Fleeting Time

Time flies on butterfly's wings.

Heart beats on musical strings.

Life's summer leaves shed from branches of trees.

Memories all become, as time forever flees.

Artwork by Shirleen Manzur

Power of Love

Decomposed, Devastated
I will rise my friends and foes.
Rise from the depths of the bellowing seas;
Rise from the quicksand and debris.

Majestic and wise,
Like an eagle I will rise.
With lightning speed, leaving the aches and pains;
Leaving the shadows of darkness and rain;

I will rise and fly through the storms.
I will pass the mountains and deserts,
Leaving all the shreds and pieces of hurt,
Rise from the torments inflicted upon;
I will not face defeat.

Born,
Not to be defeated but win.
My power of love,
My heart just won't give in.

Grass in Green

Soothe the eyes, expanse of carpeted green,
Stands tall the tiny little grass so serene.
Brown dried sickles rejoice and sing,
It's now blooming budding spring.
Tiny little butterflies spread their wings.
Heavenly green with white stars honey sweet,
Bluebells, yellow dandelions paint greener, green.
The vast plain land's ocean, waves of green,
Tender moist leaves with the muddy incense breathe;
Morning glows with dew pearls on tips of grassy pitch.
Mother Earth's bounteous grow young again.

Imagine the world's land all green,
Tufts of grass dancing happily in the breeze;
Drought and famine dries the land and freeze,
The womb of the land, sometimes wheeze;
Neighbouring green meadows healthy wind,
Comfort of abundance in plenty is redeemed.

The grass deep in the ground,

Rain flourishes and it sprouts.

A time to rest, a time to recreate

This respite all need to take

Green fir trees stand firm in chilly winter,

Even, if the grass for a time turns meander.

Strong and youthful dance with vigour,

Full of wisdom's modest fervor.

Lush green trees amid the green,

Tiny strong thriving blade of grassy green;

Mother Nature spreads happiness and peace.

A wondrous world of paradise lush green, senses
appease.

Imagine a world devoid of green.

A world half its beauty, it would seem.

Mother earth fills the world with grass in greenery.

Singing voice of time in eternity;

Passionate, voiceless prayers in rhapsody,

Thank the Giver of all this grass in green, in ecstasy.

Rain Song

Cloudy chariots move darkening the planes,
drifting clouds move in foamy feathery flames.
Dusty hot wind's airy waves slowly change,
Summer's cool breeze starts to breathe again.
Lovely birds' song on branches and trees begin,
Shining droplets of water start to drip drop and
    sing.
Trickling down flowing fountain in rhythmic song,
Green branches and trees play along.
Slowly the drizzle in rhythmic tones,
Turns into a magical heavenly song;

Laughter and joy of children on the streets,
Drenched in the rain and playing with paper boats,
    is a treat.
Colorful and bright beautiful umbrellas over the
    head,
Walk swiftly the human populace;
Heavy shower starts to pour,
Roads are empty, vacant all the walkways.

Heavenly nature all to behold,

Soft and mellow weather unfold.

Streaming water across the window-pane,

Pearly jewels of rain's domain.

Passions arise in lovers' souls,

Somewhere someone sighs and sobs.

Sweet memories of forgotten bliss,

Teardrops fall hidden in raindrops, reminisce.

Slowly the day gets brighter as it ends.

Shining Sun, seven colored rainbow bends.

Dust washed away, now a pretty sight,

Nature at its best, pure and bright.

Sparkling pearls on trees and grass,

momentary time in heaven you pass.

Life and nature start anew.

Oh, beautiful rain! I bid you, adieu!

Merciful

It spreads like wildfire.
Burns or destroys,
none does it spare:
child, youth or old,
boys, girls, women or men;

No place to hide,
halted all from flights.
Runs around the globe,
always under probe,
kills or damages, whoever it finds.

Burdened in wooden planks
fires alight, ashes to water;
six feet under,
wails and cries;

Who is next?
Isolation is best.
Infected nevertheless,
it's merciless.

It will perish,
it's for sure.
Let's all, till then
stay indoors.

God's mercy
is endless.
We will endure.

Karma

Broken fences, broken hearts,
giant walls tear you apart.

A vacuum I abhor.
Universe left in chains.
I stand a spectator:
 a tyrant
    leaves scars,
a predator
    scavenges in circles;
a victim, a fighter
    bounces back.

Karma haunts,
Karma drowns;
Karma rewards.

Forgotten Pebbles

Walking on the sea beach of life,

Rolling endless pebbles I see.

Crystal pearly waves kiss my feet.

Some pebbles roll on the sandy beach,

Some move away in watery waves.

Some I take in my hands and keep,

Some I throw;

forgotten pebbles on the seashore.

Gentle breeze soothes my being,

Caressing and tingling my flushed cheeks.

Pricking needles in my memories old;

Tears sweep through my turbulent soul.

Missing Link

I am so frightened, please take me home.
Strangers all,I won't stay here.
Raining outside we cannot roam.
You are safe here, in nurses' care.

Strangers all,I won't stay here.
Relax and let us both sing a song.
You are safe here, in nurses' care.
Let us for now both sing and play along.

Relax and let us both sing a song.
Where is my husband? He is late.
Let us for now both sing and play along;
He will come later let us wait.

Where is my husband? He is late.
My heart aches, eyes watery storm.
He will come later let us wait.
I am so frightened, please take me home.

Fractured: Rise

Battered, bruised swollen eyes,
Broken ribs, fractured thighs;

Psycho, macho powered, inferior, cold,
Depression seized tormented boar.
Frustrated, frightens the weaker soul.

New namesake damages indoors,
Patience preferred than flashing, endures;
Rising against the beastly scaffold,
Shameful acts of womenfolk.

Rise O' woman, even if you fail.
Show the light to the next woman in test.

Be the light in the darkest nights,
Be the sun in the bloodiest daylight;
Be the sun in the bloodiest of nights,
Be the fire in the darkest daylight.

Today or tomorrow the sun will shine.

Eyes Behind Masks

Oh those eyes!
Stared from behind the blue mask;
I couldn't take off my gaze.
I gazed and gazed,
my mouth stayed agape.
Lily of the Nile,
I saw the smile,
with the twinkling of her eyes.
Away in a rush, she left the bus.

Those dark black eyes
stared at night from the sky;
twinkling playful stars,
winked and smiled.

What melody sings in my heart!
Volcanic eruption, I fall apart!

If only I could see,
what lay beneath the mask!
Perhaps a beauty I have never seen?
Or perhaps the smile that could stop a million
ships;
or perhaps ……
I dare not think.

Poetry blossoms again in lovers' hearts:
coy, bold gazes, behind the kaleidoscopic masks;
Birth of poets and poems,
new stories written;
with hundreds of gazes,
mysterious eyes, shrouded faces.

Tasneem Hossain

Pawns in the Game

I.

Thundering sounds of artillery guns around.

Cries of wounded, under machine gun fire, drown.

Tanks and fighter planes bombs shelled,

Below a red canopy of human field;

Sounds of heavy boots march ahead.

Cope with extreme peril and danger, scarlet red.

Condemned, perhaps, to fight and die;

Weary of life and death under the sky,

Poison gas from far, threatens death.

Trench terror of hand-to-hand combat;

Clubs and knives, kills many in grisly raids.

Mud, blood, rats, slime, disease and rain

Turn trenches in death wells;

Pawns of the game creep, crawl, flounder and

drown.

Death's smell in dank air, darkness perceive;

Resilience motivated by comradeship,

Soldiers fight alongside friends and grieve.

Patriotism, freedom and valour

Encourage men to military service and warfare.

Terrified, seldom disobey orders to attack.

Military discipline, compels not to backtrack.

Disobeying orders, results severe,

Convicted 'deserter' faces death sentence,

Executed by own armies for military offence.

II.

Grisly images etched on conscience, senses charred;

Shell shocked pawns, land in some mental wards.

Trauma of war: a nightmare;
Cold, damp, dark walls;
Soldiers lie at home on broken beds.
Amputated hands or legs, paralysed, blinded,
Scarred hearts, live borrowed lives they dread.
Glittering medals on their cracked walls;
Victorious smiles, sparkling teeth
Of leaders on the newspapers flash.

Mindless acts of leaders' self-interests,
Lead to such human catastrophe, so sad.
They gloat in ecstasy.
The world waits for its destiny.

Intruder in My Head

An intruder in my head
came last night.
It tormented and tortured,
I could sleep no more.
It lit the candle of love
which burned brighter and bright.
The sparks travelled through veins,
my body kept awake.
Gallons of water
couldn't calm the flames.

Intruder in my head,
please go away.
O! But the thoughts and passions
are here, forever to stay.

Tasneem Hossain

You are the Reason

You don't know how much I care,
you don't know how I feel;
you don't know how my heart aches,
When you don't talk to me;
When you don't show me you are there for me.

The world seems all so bare,
Nothing to live for, or to care;
Meaningless seems all that is there.
The sun doesn't shine anymore,
The moon is all lusterless.

Sometimes I choke, I cannot breathe.
No one to tell how I feel,
All becomes useless and bleak;
Life seems to nothingness slip.
All this I repeatedly tell, but you do not believe.

One day this may happen so,
I will no more be able to live;
This tension in my heart will block,
Rhythm of life I will be so cold.

I write this poem to let you know:

You are the one who lets me breathe;

You are the one who let my life cease.

Another Sunrise

I lie in bed, my heart feebly beats.
Nurses, doctors run around
covered in masks and shields not a moment of
peace.

Behind the closed door my beloved sleeps.
We lay there fifteen days or more,
covered with oxygen masks gasping to breathe.

Now I lie here, she on the other side,
I knocked on death's door to let me in,
trade my place and let my beloved live.
Deaths' angel ignored my plea.
She lies hanging on a cliff
ready to fly to an unknown destiny.
Raindrops drizzle down my cheeks,
filled with remorse and grief.
Cobwebs in my head like empty vessels,
echo the drumbeats of marching bands.
Sounds of tinnitus shrieking bells,
screech through my ear with flames.

The myriads of color grow hazier now:
only pitch black and gleaming white.

Far in the darkness, shining fireflies;
starlit carpet from moonlight spreads to welcome
the bride.

Calm tranquility reigns in moonlight;
tomorrow there will be another sunrise.

Tasneem Hossain

I am a Prostitute

Dazzling a smile, through cheap lipstick I wink,
Making the onlookers drool and blink;
Adorned in tight skirts with slits,
Low necked blouse and tight fitted jeans,
Painted nails with matching high heels.
Let the lechers know what I mean.
Don't care what others may think,
I am a 'leper' or a 'dirty chick'.

Drenched in strong perfume I let the beggars beg.
Drown in oblivion, I take too many pegs.
Crying in the rain, filled with filth
Washing away my so called sins and silt;

O you great passersby!
Don't you dare judge me or even try,
For little do you know how I came here and why.
I was for them just a costly good to supply.

However much I shriek or cry,
Here my freedom is denied.
These are not the choices I have made,
I am a slave of human trade.

Before My Light Goes Out

Before my light goes out, let me rejoice.
Dance in the rain under the wet sky,
tip toe on the white flaky snow flurries that
beautify;
Bathe in the golden rays of sunny sky high.

Let me celebrate the wonders of nature.
Let me feel all divinity around.
Let me enjoy the gifts of God.
Let me bathe in heavenly love.

Let me rejoice each moment as it flies.
Blessed are we with all that is bestowed on us.

Life's Journey

Crystal pearly watery waves
In a never-ending gentle caress,
Take my body in the dark abyss and bliss.
I drift like a straw in airy space,
Speck of dust on the sands of life's deserted path;
Drifting driftwood tumbling in sea waves,
Lazing on the windswept beaches where oceans
reign.

Today or tomorrow we will die,
This world to another we will survive.
What lies is only the mortal remain,
Swiftly flies the soul to the sky's haven.

Life's journey never does cease.
Smile and live in eternal peace.

I Will Not Accept Defeat

My life starts with apprehensions in the mother's
womb,
Birth of a girl means it will be a doom.
Prayers not a daughter but a glorious boy,
Curse for the household will be this unlucky ploy.

A woman is nothing but a naughty decoy;
Opportunist was beautiful Helen of Troy.
Mischievous and dark natured when girls do
bloom,
In secrets my destiny will be an earthy tomb.

To wear the crown,
They think men are with tricks won and drown.
Women, you frown, are at fault always;
My life is forever ablaze.

Stormy winds seldom seize,

My life is always a lease.

The wrath of a woman she keeps hidden for

peace,

My fight for justice will never cease.

Start the countdown,

I am not going to breakdown;

No matter how big the fleet,

I will not accept defeat.

Proud to be the woman, you see.

Your home is heaven, it's because of me.

Heaven in Your Arms

Dark is the night, sky is bright.
The world sleeps in silvery moonlight;
Wafting winds whisper your name,
They kiss my cheeks again and again;

I reach for the moon and embrace,
Silvery sparkle spread all over earth's face;
Tears now pearls of memories surround,
Sighs, now whispers of love whirl me around;

Light of your love shines in your eyes,
All my tomorrows are forever yours, sweet
    lullabies;
Memories of our love will never grow old.
Times of our love will shine forever my love.

The joy of my heart ceaselessly storms.
I find my heaven here in your arms.

The Devil Inside

A devil in my head
goes scratch, scratch, scratch.
It's nails claw inside my brain
and lets it bleed.

The palms play loud:
thump, thump, thump.
A strong headache,
it jabs on the skull.
I go dizzy.
The devil inside says
'Go, play foul and evil.'

The flowing blood
tries to cool it down.
Cells go crazy play havoc,
It's so insane

Reason argues,
Emotion pleads;
The fire inside
burns me alive.

Brace up

Kaleidoscopic views from 160 feet above.
Moon on roofs, no more races behind cars;
moonlight splashes between brick wall gaps.

Trees are not barren, nor seen.
Demolished for buildings, fences,
chairs and ornamental pieces-
       we gasp for more oxygen.

Friends seldom meet.
We are so busy
running after fame and money.
       Life is barren like trees.

Still the sun shines each day.
Hopes and desires play hide and seek.
Halfway down the grave
       we realise the meaning of life.

Colourful kaleidoscopes-
frustrations and heartaches:
It's too late.

Infancy
is all white.
Brace up for the eternal wave.

Tasneem Hossain

Reflections

Far away from the crowd,
far from the glaring chaos;
out of the blaring car horns,
out of the shrieks of loneliness,
out of all the madness that surrounds;
Out of the city, out of the cacophony
I chose to go and find solace.

I lay on the bench in the park.
The red Krishnochura smiled,
spreading beauty and love around.
The cuckoos on the trees sang to me.
The Banyan tree above lazed, gave me shade.
The winds whispered lullabies,
crickets and grasshoppers chirped in harmony.
The bright blue sky enveloped
all with light and energy.
The white heavenly sky angels danced for me.

The two little tattered barefoot children
laughed and played,
brightening life with joyous laughter.

Echoes of their laughter spoke to me.
Don't you see?
Don't you hear?
Within the boundaries of the broken walls,
open your inner eyes to the universe.
Nature waits for positive affirmations.
The lovely essence of beautiful thoughts;
The peace you desire waits to be discovered.
Happiness lies only within.

Feelings

I see you in visions, I feel your pain.
You never share or even care,
Your pain and torments are for me a bane;
Your distress I feel, send you a prayer.

Friends we are, close at heart
Feelings grow stronger, closer every day.
Feel the pain and happiness all the same,
Parting goodbyes may happen any day.

Chance and destiny make people's paths cross.
Meeting strangers may sometimes be a part.
Why it happened with us: I am at a loss.
Friends we became and then we depart.

If some day, somewhere, we cross our ways,
Will you remember me in any way?

Sandcastle of Time

I stood on the sandcastle of time,
My foothold strong;
Never looked back,
Marched ahead with pride;

Crushed all against my tide,
Innocent lives ruined on the line.
Powerful, fleeing, all on the run.
Nothing could stop me under the sun

The sandcastle grew smaller,
My time on the race grew weaker;
Crumbled on the ground.
What good did it do?

Now I am dust under the ground.

The Playwright

Memories may bring smiles and tears both- you
sigh.
You may smile, your eyes never lie.
Sweet sad memories keep dancing in the
moonlight,
Today you may be passing twilight.
Tomorrow you may be in the limelight,
Never be afraid of the spotlight.
Life keeps moving.

God is the playwright.

Wasted Love

Tossed and turned,
Her whole world went wrong.
He meant no harm,
But harsh words raged on.
Tears swelled up,
Her heart bled on.
He begged forgiveness,
She had never asked.
Nothing gave respite,
Her breath felt tight.

Ignored and hurt,
It broke her heart.
Love for him ,
She couldn't forget;
She cared and prayed for him
to overcome his distress.

He didn't care,

For him, no time to spare;

For he was a king,

by all means.

Fake friends and followers plenty.

She prayed always,

left him alone;

for this way

she could not go on.

Her heartaches remained,

she wouldn't forget.

Life goes on for him.

Ghost of a life, she moves away

to a far distant land.

Her heart she leaves behind.

He lost his crown,
no one around;
Pain and heartache,
memories flash back;
the pure innocent face,
tears in eyes, smile on face;
Prayers and wishes come pouring
In his mind.

He lost the jewel
in quest of fame.

Calls and connects.

'I am sorry, she was buried today.
She left a note, professed her love for you'

His heart beats faster,
breath he can hold no longer;
drops on the floor.
Smiles, for he knows
she waits for him on the other side.

Tasneem Hossain

Life of Romelu Lukaka

Yes, that's me on the bench,

waiting for my turn;

yet no one calls my name.

I go home. Ma gives milk,

mixes water in it.

My father is broke,

we have to manage on our own.

I don't say a word,

lest it makes her stressed.

Eating my lunch I promise myself,

to ease her life from this distress.

Ma borrows bread from the bakers,

Promises to pay them later.

The baker know us;

So lets her take a loaf: no fuss.

I come home and see my mom cry,
she wipes her tears and sighs.

'Mum, it's gonna change,' I say.
'Don't worry much it's gonna be okay.

I was six.

I promise myself, to make her happy one day.
I play and play, till my body starts to ache.
I sit on the same bench every day,
waiting for a chance for me to play;

One, two, three an injury!

No one around.
To call me, they are bound;
Five, six, seven a rebound;
I shoot the ball.
Straight it goes and a goal!
Eight, nine, ten I am back again.

Wearing dad's shoes, I'm in the team.
I play with zest, we start to win.

Grandpa calls, 'Promise me boy.
You will look after my daughter always.'

I promise, 'I will someday.'
'

Soon in the league,
I am the goal freak.
Lose the final game,
still I have made my name.

Wanted by the teams,
I am a striker in the field.

Now,
We live in a house, where rats don't scurry;
pure milk to drink; eat rice and curry.

Grandpa, see? My mum is happy?
Everything's okay.
I kept my promise
Alas! Grandpa is in heaven.

I am proud, I kept my promise.
I'm Belgian Romelu Lukaka.

Found Poetry based on an interview by Belgiun striker
Romelu Lukaka to *The Players' Tribune* on June 18, 2018.

https://www.theplayerstribune.com/articles/romelu-lukaku-ive-got-some-things-to-say

Madness

Twelve seconds…

Crash!
Splintered glass,
Smashed windows;

Crowds around
Click, click, click,
Posts on Facebook;

No one cares
to pick up the pieces
of the wounded.

A beggar in clutches
sits on the road;
calls for help on a broken phone.

Teardrops
Roll down my cheeks.
Bleeding body,
Wounded womb;

Go share your posts,
Collect acclaims;
Pitiless frames,
Humanity ceases existence.

Compassion

Heart is a geometrical meshed lyre.
Ignored and hurt, perceived as barbed wire.
Neglect and absence char a loving heart,
never mends to its original form of art.

A heart that chars with neglect burns very fast.
Burns to ashes and dust at last.
Frozen hearts never melt,
know that they only break.

Meaningless quarrels give rise to distance.
Unfold, untold, passive resistance.
Differences burn, sometimes, relations apart.
Ashes, dust and frozen broken hearts.

Rootless relationships slowly dissolve,
cause only frustrations and discord.

A heart that cares and loves with no selfish
  desires,
needs to be nurtured with a little love and care.
Life is meaningful,
with compassion beautiful.

The Sweet Thief

That thief steals into your heart.
One moment it's ecstasy,
The next, it wrenches and tears you apart;
Life seems heavenly; next it's hell.

None can perceive when it comes,
Whom it touches or where it prods;
How it creeps in, how it crawls.
That sweet little thief, that we call love.

Take Me Home to My Baby

Who are you? Can you tell me true?

Where is my baby? Please bring her to me.

    This is me, mom your daughter Sue.

    Look at me, hold me tight. Sit safely.

Where is my baby? Please bring her to me.

My head is a buzz. Don't make a fuss.

    Look at me, hold me tight.Sit safely.

Are you the nurse? Please bring my purse.

My head is a buzz. Don't make a fuss.

Why is everything so hazy?

Are you the nurse? Please bring my purse.

    It's me, mom, your baby. Don't be so hasty.

Why is everything so hazy?

Please take me home to my baby girl Sue.

    It's me, mom, your baby. Don't be so hasty.

Who are you? Can you tell me true?

Break the Bias

Who is a woman? Who is a woman to you?
Your mother, sister, wife, daughter, friend or, a
colleague?
The mother brought you to the world, raised you.
The sister? Looks after you, plays with you, fights
for you.
The wife goes through thick and thin.
To the daughter, you are her prince.
The friend? Who listens to you when you are in
grief.
The colleague, who supports you to win.

Yet, she withers with time, alas!
Decorated in hair or some vase.
You hold a bias against the woman, a human
being.
Weak? Strong enough, to endure bone breaking
pain
to give birth to you and me.
Wisdom is her trait, for she knows how to teach
you life and lead.

A river of intelligence and wisdom flows through
    her beautiful being.
Give her the freedom she fully deserves.
Equal opportunities so she can prove her worth,
to share with you her thoughts,
her choices, her decisions equally heard.
A world where she is treated equally no matter
    what;
to make this wonderful world a heavenly earth.

So today, right now,
break the bias, when you see a daughter in the
    womb.
Before she is born, don't make her an earthy tomb.

Break the bias, when you let your son free in the
    fields play.
While your daughter toils in the kitchen, I pray.
Break the bias, when you say, "Don't go out, stay
    home.
You will be married off soon any day."

Break the bias, give her education.

Break the bias, the way you look at a woman.

She is not a commodity or a good.

She is a human being just like you and me.

She is equal - treat her equally.

Once empowered, she empowers you more.

The world is cruel, to let her in peace dwell.

A woman scorned, with broken heart, dashed
  dreams and fallen hopes.

Not left alone - to live her life as her own.

Respect the differences in her with you.

Let her voice be heard without oppression, fear, or
  scorn.

When tides are mellow, she is soft.
When in need, a strong maiden she is!
Let her thrive to be bold and brave.
Remove all biases on her race, colour, age, body
  type.
Remove all biases of her place and society alike.
Embrace her sufferings as your own.

Will you be the first to stop the bias and change?
Change your outlook on women in disparity,
gender discrimination for the world to gain?
Stand and honour women in solidarity?

Let the fire, the light within her shine.
Let the world thrive with her worth enshrined.

Be the champions to break the bias.
Be the champions to break the bias.

Eternal Life

Sun may shine today or tomorrow decline,
light of sun it holds inside;
shining brighter, it will forever rise.

Thunderstorms darken the blue sky above,
clouds and lightening covers, blanket of gloom;
the blue sky forever shines anew.

The moon eclipses, covered with darkness soon;
sun's love lightens, glows fully bright the new
moon
dazzling the dark sky in silvery bloom.

The never-ending water of oceans flow,
wombs of the oceans forever with water grow;

Tsunami's tidal waves drown the earth below,
Earth with nature's abundance, surfaces
    meadows.

Small gestures of friendship, love, and blessings
meaningful moments of happiness remain;
small miracles happen in different forms.
Dreams come true, we transform.

Time may fly, one may die.
The soul forever in heaven flies.

Mother

Sometime it hurts,
to see faces all vibrant;
talking of mother's love.
Knew no one whom I could call my mother,
separated when ten months old.

Brought up by grannies and aunts,
school days would drag on.
Mothers with smiles and pride in eyes would
come,
laughter and happiness would abound;
I sat on a chair with no one around,
thinking how it would be if my mom was around;

Days, months, and years passed.
My father, my angel, cared with undying love.
Then the day of my wedding came.
Decked in jewelry and gorgeous dress,
went to another home that became my new home.

Two years went by, then the news:
I was going to be a mother soon.
Vibrations in my womb I felt,
tiny feet and hands I held.

Then this little child was born.
Most wonderful day when,
I held the baby boy in my arms.
I held him close to my heart;
nothing seemed more precious more than this.
Emotions swelled never known before,
fruits of motherhood I tasted with all aplomb.

Once again, nine months passed.
A little baby girl with bright eyes was born.
Nurtured both with affection and care;
A handsome son and beautiful daughter, what a
    pair!

Days, months, and years passed.
my babies grew up into wonderful swans.
Happiness in my life with them I found,
felt the love of a mother wrap me around;
With their caring love, peace I found.

Fame

Fame
is a flickering moment.
So shine,
shine until it ends.

A firefly
shines and dims,
shines again.
After the rain comes
rainbow,
vanishes again;
appears in the sky again.

Memories of glory remain
carved in heart
forever shining inside.

Shine, shine, shine
deep inside;
nothing can destroy
those moments of bliss.

Everything Comes Back

A speck of dust in the vast sea
washed away by the huge tidal waves....
stays buried under the ocean.
Centuries pass,
stays there,
a silent spectator;
waiting to return.

Again it rises from the womb.
Flows with the waves and reaches the shore.
Nothing gets lost,
Everything comes back.
In another name, another place;
another form.

New existence.

Forever

Watering a plant keeps flowering bright,
Nourish it and it blooms alright.
Deprive and it will not thrive.
Dried branches, brown leaves devoid of blossoms
    survive.

One day you will miss me, I am sure.
Emotions by then will dry, though love is pure.
No matter how you cry,
The blossoms of tree you will see dry.

Senile one day we all become,
To old age we all succumb.
Fair weather friends always in great times meet;
Loving, caring friends at the end you surely need.

Treat well whom you least expect that day.
The broken, loving heart you will find forever stay.

Tasneem Hossain

Mother in Disguise

I held you in my womb,
felt your every move.
A soft, small bundle I held in my arms.
You made me cry and laugh with your sweet silly
    charms.

God whispered in my ears,
'This is your gift forever to keep.'
The gift from heaven made me weep in bliss.

I saw you grow: a blossoming flower
spreading fragrance of love, compassion and care.
Tackling life's puzzles with amazing flair;
sports, dance, literature, math,
economics or physics nothing did you spare.

Amazing talent, yet, so gentle and fair.
Humbly you treat all with respect, which is rare.
You bring tears of happiness in my eyes,
smiles on my face of joy and pride.

Graceful symbol of piety,

taking care of me;

you are a beautiful deity.

I love you my daughter- a wonderful surprise.

God has sent me my mother in disguise.

Free

Free from the darkness of your soul.
I rejoice in freeing my spirit, enthrall.
Desires and whims fulfilled,
That's only what you wished.
Never cared for the passionate love,
Never thought about the tortured heart;

Today you cursed and cursed alone.
Not giving a moment to defend my own.
Diseased mind of your darkened soul,
Blaming without recourse or console;
Silently I listened lest you be perturbed.

Momentary stillness and then the light;
I found my heavy heart take its flight.
Saw the lust in your love's eyes.
Love shackles chained, slowly loosened.
Shocked, I saw the other side, saddened.

A person forever in your own little world,
Uncaring for any other soul;
Hidden ugly face beneath the mask.
A devil under that filthy glass;
The devil residing in you, I saw at last.

Hatred never, but pity born,
Felt for you poor evil soul;
Chained forever faking love troll.

My heart free began to fly and soar.
Free now I am from any remorse.

I Wish

I wish I had never fallen in love
with that sweet naughty smile of yours.
I wish my heart had never felt
the strong vibrating articulation of your voice.
I wish you had never looked at me
with those black beautiful eyes,
penetrating into mine.

The smile whispers to me to be in your arms,
The voice echoes in my thoughts.
The eyes lure me towards your heart;
neither can I ignore, nor can I forget.
It grows stronger every day,
leaving me to sway in a sweet sad ballet.

I don't want to swim to the shore,
nor do I want to drown.
Magnetic black eyes make me linger in space.
Your smile like the rays of sun keeps me awake.
Like the rumbling thunder of lightening,
your voice has become a part of mine.

How I wish I had not known you

Because my love, this love will only drown my
soul.

Fallen in grace, I will depart.

My embrace leaving no impact on your playful
heart.

Life in a Teacup

All in a teacup.

Green tea good for health.
Black tea bitter, not my cup of tea.
Milk tea tasty, not so healthy.
White tea- losing weight is beauty.

Some teas come with sweetness, some bitter
    sweet;
Some bland, tasteless, some refreshing in
    essence.

Some of us leave with only a sip,
Some a little, some half a mile,
Sometimes a long journey till it ends.

Life's journey halts at some place.
The cup of life empties wherever it ends.

Memories of bitter taste, leaves scars and pains;
Thoughts of the sweet one's taste with love
  remains.

Choose your cup of tea wisely.

Confession

The heartaches I can feel and touch.

Voices of silence share the pain and agony clutch.

Mindless whispers shriek and beg to say,

Vibrant passions I need to convey.

Taboo to speak, yet emotions so fierce;

Heart needs to breathe but pierce.

Burning passions of the soul now a curse,

Flaming emotions but no one to console;

Each cell of the flowing blood,

Speaks of my love and affection;

Carved in flesh its full existence,

Merges in eternal universe,

Voices the melody of love;

Let go, I cannot do.

How can I let go? I love you.

Love

You sit there and sleep on the bench.
Drifting winds kiss your face, I wrench.
Silvery waves of auburn red,
flow like sea waves across airy space.

I, on the opposite bench, lie and look.
Thousands of storms passing my brook;
wafting kisses gently touch my lips,
tenderly my heart writes thousands of scripts.

The whistling engine gives a blow.
Kaleidoscopic colors swirl in sunlight and glow.

Life

God has given everything a place to grow,
Even if it is small, even if it snows;
Nature always glows.
Life like a stream always flows

Memories

If I left you, would you cry for me?
If I never come back again
Would you go searching for me?

When it rains, when it's night
Do you remember me?
Do you ever feel my touch?

The days would linger and you would wait.
Wait for the calls and look me in my eyes.
Do you remember any of those days?

Do you ever look back,
To the days we had together?
Or have you forgotten me altogether?

Memories hidden in heart cry out.
Rain starts pouring from the clouds.
Sounds of fleeting time forever goes cling clang
    clang.

Tasneem Hossain

Lover's World

Thunderstorm lashes chilly angry blows.
Tumultuous sea waves and oceans growl,
Impassioned night crawlers run fast and troat;
Passionate love's breathing dances and floats.

Wandering clouds feel misty watery eyes,
Ready to fall through dark, grey, cloudy skies;
Heartbeats travel across oceans and seas,
Lost travellers feel rhythmic motion in breeze.

Light comes shining through the depth of
    darkness.
Thoughts float through the rhythm of nothingness,
Silence sings its own solitary tune
Mellow music of heart pierces the gloom.

You are the light of my heart's home.
Looking at you I see my wondrous world.

Motherhood

Young or old, doesn't matter at all.
Mothers, daughters, sisters most women folk
to motherhood transform;
Life on earth breathes with heavenly love;
Celebrations for Motherhood in all spheres above
    all.

Penitence

I wish I could look in your eyes,
see what's in your mind,
if you feel the same too;

Distances are there, we are so far
miles apart;
yet you seem so near
close to my heart.
Mountains or rivers
cannot let my feelings cease.

I wish you knew,
how I feel your absence.
How much it hurts,
not seeing you is insane.
My feelings for you
with time is growing more intense.
Leaving this world
not letting you know would be a penitence.

Poetry Teacher

You're quite a soul of perfection.
Great teacher, full of affection;
Taught with zest and smile,
Admiration, students could seldom hide;

Different times, different forms,
Poetry for us to reform;
Epics, sonnets, triolet , pantoum,
free verse, ballad, villanelle and haiku
New grounds to pursue;
We all thank you.

Tasneem Hossain

Wonderful World

I lost a friend today.
Perhaps you lost one yesterday.
Maybe you, many of the last decade.
Right now, maybe you are in front of a death bed.

Life is just moving air in space,
Breathing through in a relay race;
Reaching destinations out of nothingness;
Or is it actually life's fulfillment?

We come for vacation a minute or a day,
Clawing at each other, travelling the hard way;
Easier it would be, If we moved hand in hand,
Loved each other with no regrets;

Disappear we will all from this space, friend or foe.
Let's make our world with love aglow.
We can all save our souls,
From damnation to salvation for all;

Jealousy, hatred competitions apart,
Love, compassion free for all we can start.
What a beautiful world it will be,
If we try, eternal peace there will be!

I wrote this poem when one of my university friends Flora passed away.

Music in Poems

Like it or not my poems rhyme.
Music in life, rhyming is my style.
Go on,
come with a sword and stab me with your knife,
I will not run for my life.

Music everywhere, I embrace.
Melody in poems has its grace.

Life - A Lesson in Poetry

Life in verse:
We all immerse.
Marks many contrasts,
students form a collage.
Diversity and intensity,
a montage;
rhythm of poetry lasts.
Knowledge is forever vast.

Stages of Love

Love, they say, does many a wondrous things;
Love also damages and destroys one's whole
  being.

One can fall in love in teens or twenties
It can happen at forty, sixty or eighty.
Only feelings and attraction vary.

In teens or twenties, scared and young you have a
  fire;
At forty, you are wiser and fair;
At sixty, you care and say a prayer.
At eighty, you look for a friend, a companion.

Sometimes love is a heavenly gift;
Sometimes it brings destruction and grief.

Situations change according to age;
Situations change according to name and place.
Whatever the reason or situation,
It can happen anytime.

Love is sometimes heaven;
Love is sometimes damnation.

Passions arise in many kinds.
It's a beautiful thing,
Until you commit a sin.
Think of it and be wise.

Tasneem Hossain

Will You?

Will you miss me when I'm not near?
Look at the stars in the flickering moonlight?
Will you remember me when I'm not there?

The rainbow, the sky nothing will disappear.
Will you still lie on the beach in silvery nights?
Will you miss me when I'm not near?

World's merry go round will keep circling,
sun keep shining brightly, only I won't be here.
Will you remember me when I'm not there?

The life that we shared is very rare.
Lover's world, full of delight;
Will you miss me when I'm not near?

The world's tribulations aren't fair.
Holding hands we braved the plights.
Will you remember me when I'm not there?

Will you remember to send me a prayer?
Teardrops fall to the ground, hazy is my sight.
Will you miss me when I'm not near?
Will you remember me when I'm not there?

The Eagle

The wide blue sky is its domain.
High Mountain tops are where it rests.
Wide wings open from its chest,
The golden eagle then looks its best.
Flies high far from human vision,
Sharp eyes with near perfect precision;
Free it is, mighty lord of the sky
Freedom is its birthright, majestic is its flight.

The eagle perched on the tree,
Looked down, ravenous eyes: its spirit free.
Looking for prey, spotted one with glee;
Quick flapping wings swooped down, lest it flee
Caught in feet, took off victoriously;

The small little creature wiggled and wiggled.
Its struggle didn't help but made it cripple.
The eagle, mighty monarch of the realms
Landed on the high mountains to enjoy its meal;

Today, as it swooped to have its feast
Struggled in its fight against its prey, its treat;
Mighty it seems but now its flight is weak;
Broken wings, age withers even the mightiest
    beings.

Fell with a thud, who soared the skies flying free.
Wriggling in pain its last minutes in agony;
A giant shadow falls and darkens all,
Stares with eyes now dimming, life's last call;

Flying angel with wide wings of endless grace.
Soars majestically with wings open from the chest;
The golden eagle then looks its best.

The progeny now flies through the open space,
Defying sun and floats high above stormy winds;

A calm and peaceful death now it may embrace.
Life goes on with amazing grace.

About the Author

Tasneem Hossain is a Bangladeshi multi-lingual poet who shares time between Bangladesh and Canada. She completed her Masters in English Language and Literature from Dhaka University in 1986. Her wanderings in other areas of literature include fiction, translation, academic pieces, columns, and op-eds. She writes in English, Bangla, and Urdu. Her writings appear in magazines, different dailies, nd annual publications of different countries. To name a few: *ternational Human Rights Art Festival 2022 Anthology: Tyranny nchained; Woman's Freedom, Borderless Journal* (Singapore), *scover Mississauga and More* - eBook (Canada), *Krishnochura* nited Kingdom), *EDAS Chronicle, The Dhaka Literature, An Ekushey nthology, The Daily Star, bdnews24.com*, and *Asian Age Online* angladesh).

er publications consist of *The Pearl Necklace* and *Floating Feathers oetry),* and *Split and Splice (article).*

e runs a project named *Life in Verses* where she conducts poetry iting workshops.

e is the Director of Continuing Education Centre (human capacity velopment organization). As a training consultant her expertise lies Communication Management and Language. She worked as faculty nglish Language) in Chittagong University of Engineering and chnology. She also worked as newscaster, commentary reader, and dio jockey in radio Bangladesh for 10 years. She directed akespeare's play *A Midsummer Night's Dream.*

Comments by Readers

"*The Pearl Necklace* will provide people unique insight about the beauty of social relationships through a collection of eye opening poems. Thank you for your eloquent contributions to literature at home and abroad."
- Doly Begum, MPP, Canada

"It's nice to see the beautiful literary creation of modern-day English scholar, Tasneem Hossain, from the land of Rabindra Nath Tagore. Not only, Sarojini Naido, and Kamal Surraya Das, but another daughter of the East writes in modern English today. It seems that, after a century, the soul of Indian born Rudyard Kipling speaks through the voice of Tasneem."
- Manzar H. Akbar, Physician, Cardiologist, Iran

"Tasneem Hossain's collections of poems invite contemplation, appreciation and understanding about the exquisiteness of nature, create awareness about society, portray human emotions and highlight human responsibilities. The rhythm and choice of words combine brilliant imagery. Each word counts with linguistic turns, skillful line breaks and use of alliteration and metaphors. Her poems are deep and beautiful. *The Pearl Necklace* is a must read over and over again."
- Farhana Haque Rahman, Executive Director, IPS Inter Press Service, Canada

"Whatever Tasneem Hossain depicts becomes vital to exploring meaning of life in our otherwise occupied consciousness. And her diction makes the subjects, be it myriad facets of nature, or our tears smiles, and sighs, come so alive that her poetry, in effect, verges on a visual art. Her poems inspire emotions and are crafted in soulful words. Both stir the hearts of many to pause, think and feel a

newed urge for life. A stellar example of how simple words can aft profound feelings into a beautiful piece of poetry."
- Reja Syed Ali, Literary Critic, Bangladesh

s a poet, Tasneem Hossain bears a pensive elegance of nderstanding the personal, emotional, and social worlds where we e in. And thus, her poems captivate any sentient reader because of e thoughtful, lyrical attire they wear. Her poetic persona, admittedly, elps us to discover the equally poetic reader residing within urselves. Her poems are a lyrical journey of sensitivity and ntemplation."
- Faheem H. Shahed,PhD, Academic & Writer, Bangladesh

asneem Hossain's poems are a wonderful work of art with rhyme nd rhythm in harmony; philosophical depth and practical imagery. In is age of surrealistic writings, her poems bring us back to reality. ostly ending on a hopeful note, a subtle touch of spiritualism is also oticeable in her poems."
- Shirleen Manzur, Researcher, Canada

asneem Hossain I'm waiting for your next book to hit the shelves. a time when there's so much anger and hurt in the world, reading ur poems has a calming effect. A beautiful change. Thank you for at."
- Ian Ross, Accountant, Canada

asneem, you are a person with a beautiful soul and your poems ve the same reflection of beauty within.... now a person who knows u (like me) doesn't have to look twice to find the harmony between e poems and the cover pictures of your books."
- Farhana Hossain, Physician and an avid reader, Bangladesh

Other Works by Tasneem Hossain

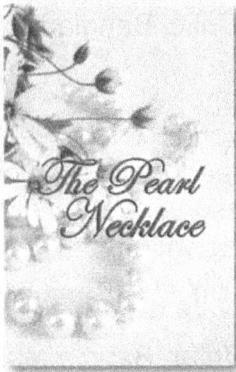

Poetry to Tasneem Hossain is an ever-flowing river reflecting all that surrounds us. *The Pearl Necklace* is a lyrical journey of sensitivity and contemplation through life in its different colors and shades. The title poem is about unfulfilled true love. *The Invisible Cord* is a celebration of mother's love. *Agony* is a cry for social justice. The last poem *The Lighthouse* ends with an aspiration to make our existence more meaningful. The essence of her poems is the beauty of nature and human life.

https://forms.gle/4JdcJi792ZSZS63R7

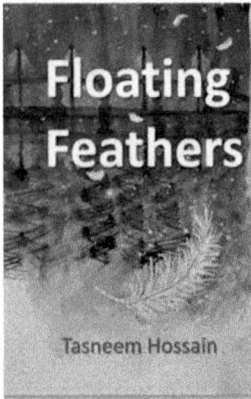

The poems of Tasneem Hossain's *Floating Feathers* are an outcome of the spiraling moments of her emotional outbursts. The title poem is a confession of the poetic thoughts floating and falling into her lap. *Let's Walk Together, You and I* deals with old age agonies and pains of becoming senile. Human emotions, social justice, kindness towards humanity and transience of life are some of the themes of her poetry. At the end there is a collection of haiku poems.

https://forms.gle/4JdcJi792ZSZS63R7

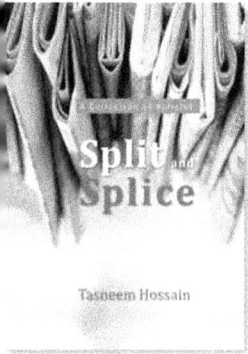

Tasneem Hossain's book *Split and Splice* is a compilation of some of the writer's articles published in different newspapers dealing with historical events and interesting facts about different issues, some are about acquiring good habits for a peaceful and successful life, some discuss ways of improving lifestyles and overall well-being having relevance to day-to-day life. The different aspects of life will help readers to become more conscious of life and the world surrounding them.

https://forms.gle/4JdcJi792ZSZS63R7

www.ingramcontent.com/pod-product-compliance
Lightning Source LLC
Chambersburg PA
CBHW071816020426
42331CB00007B/1498